Published by

GoTellSomeOne.com

I0426575

What Is Your BIG IDEA?

How We Reunited

JACK BAUER

With His TV Family

Ryan T. Richardson, BA LLB

For our Grandkids,

The Biggest Ideas
I Ever Met

=

"Don't publish this. You don't have my permission."

Janice Richardson
(Harpist)

Before we begin...

- This is designed to be a quick read, but be warned - it is full of **Live Links** to fascinating and engaging content.

- **80-85%** was written on my phone.

- This book is offered for free! Please share with anyone you know who could use a "Reboot" after the last few years.

- If you have been encouraged by this book and want to "pay-what-it's-worth-to-you", any contribution will be appreciated and will help us achieve our next **Big Idea**!

Aim your camera if you choose to
"pay-what-it's-worth-to-you".

*Thank you and I hope this helps
you find Your Big Idea!*

"Hi. I am Ryan and I run my mouth for a living."

That is my elevator speech. If that phrase is new to you, an elevator speech is a short intro that you give in social or business settings that takes as little time as possible.

You may notice that my definition of an elevator speech was longer than my elevator speech.

Your elevator speech is ideally designed to quickly summarize you, and also encourage more questions from your audience. It is meant to be a conversation starter.

At this point in my life, I realize that my stock in trade is Conversations, Big Ideas and Nostalgia. And it's only taken 50 years to come to that conclusion!

But my elevator speech is brief and absolutely true. I started my career in hospitality and retail, branched into the practice of law, followed by digital marketing, adding **teaching and public speaking** across the country. (Somewhere in there, I worked at a funeral home, which is a whole other book by itself.)

Each role that we take on adds to the repertoire and makes us

~~CooCoo for Cocoa Puffs~~ more marketable and well-rounded.

Each of those endeavours require me to run my mouth.

It wasn't until the world stopped until I had to re-calibrate and merge all of those diverse skills in order to survive.

The Big Ideas I come by naturally. Both of my parents raised me to be a Big Idea person. My Mom made sure that we lived like kings and queens on a shoestring, and my Dad was always hustling.

Kids, hustling used to be a bad

word, but now we recognize that having a side hustle is a good thing. My Dad was way ahead of his time. When you are raised that way, you wonder "why doesn't everybody have a Big Idea"?

When I realized early is this - not everyone has a Big Idea and that's OK.

But I need a Big Idea always.

What is this Big Idea? I am glad that you asked.

This book is about one of my **Big Ideas**.

"24 is like water, if it gets on you, it's on you."

Aaron Michael Waldo
(24 Universe)

"That's about the worst idea I've heard of in my life!"

Bob Cochran
(Co-Father of "24")

November 5, 2021

I am less than 24 hours away from hosting a worldwide convention, featuring over 40 panellists from eight different time zones and attendees from 22 different countries. I am functioning on little to no sleep in the last week because I've been Googling and YouTubing "how to run an international convention using Zoom webinars".

My days are now spent confirming registrations, making sure that the panellists know where they're supposed to be and which time zone to be there, and generally just going out of my mind. This day is spent with many visions of me the following day, curled up in a corner, hugging a warm blanket while the convention (and also my credibility) descends into complete chaos.

And for the first time, I understand the Eminem lyric:

His palms are sweaty, knees weak, arms are heavy,
There's vomit on his sweater already, mom's spaghetti,
He's nervous, but on the surface he looks calm and ready...

Exaggerating? Not at all.

Let me back this up to give it some context. In 2002, I, like millions of people around the world got hooked on **"24"**. To be clear, **"24"** is not an illegal substance, it is a "highly addictive TV show with a pulse". If you have not heard this phrase describing a show, that is because it is the only one of its kind.

"24" features Actor/Producer Kiefer Sutherland as "Jack Bauer" and the most talented and gracious cast in existence, telling a story in Real Time. The evidence of the show's unique approach is that, in 20 years, no other television production has attempted to repeat the Real Time experience.

Not one.

As a healthily obsessed aficionado of the show, I lost so much sleep catching up with Jack Bauer and the Counter Terrorist Unit (CTU) team, as they repeatedly averted global catastrophe while the World slept peacefully, unaware of the danger they had been spared.

Let us cut back to my Dad for a minute. As a true People Person, my Dad remembered important dates and anniversaries and birthdays. Dad always carried a day timer, not a phone with all his calendar and notes, an actual Day Timer-brand Day Timer. It wasn't until he had passed on, that I realized just how much detail he would put into the day timer. In addition to the important dates mentioned, he would write down every sporting event his kids and grandkids participated in, where he ate and how much he tipped, who he called and met, daily to-do lists and seemingly insignificant details about his day.

Now that he's moved on ahead of us, every detail he wrote down is significant to me. I own about a decade of his Day Timers, and you'll have to pry them from my dead hands before I'd give them up. (Not a challenge, just a warning.)

So, because I value anniversary dates and their significance, I had a **Big Idea**, over 10 years ago. One of my theories is that everybody has a Con. As I said, not everybody has a Big Idea, but everybody has a **Con**.

Don't think you do?

What is that band, actor, singer, author, leader, celebrity, politician, preacher, cause, event that would cause you to drop this book right now, if you had the chance to meet, hang out with or attend?

I know you instantly had an answer.

That's your Con.

"When my son was 5, we got in my car, drove across the country & started seeing baseball games. We saw every stadium in the country by the time he was 7."

Matt Bissonette
(Elton John Band,
The Reddcoats)

"I went from 'will they sue me?' to 'they're passing my around my book as they write the show.'"

Steven Keslowitz
(Why You Better Call Saul)

I was watching a documentary about the ComicCon phenomenon. People travel thousands of miles for the chance to briefly meet their favorite celebrities. I remember thinking, why on earth would you do that?

And then, I remembered my "24" addiction. I knew that I would travel great distances to listen to the cast tell stories about the show.

(Confession: I enjoy listening to directors and actors commentary. I've always enjoyed the behind-the-scenes accounts of films, historical events, music, etc.)

I realized in that moment that "24" was at least one of my Cons.

But, there was no Con(vention) for Fans of "24"?

I would create one!

The first step? **Ask. Ask. Ask.**

Of all my Big Ideas, this was the most ambitious. So somehow, 10 years ago, I got a contact for "24" Director <u>Jon Cassar</u> (The Orville, Forsaken). We will talk more about Jon later.

Out of the blue, I sent Jon a quick proposal as to why the world needed a Convention for fans of Jack Bauer and the "24" series. Especially as it reached its 10th anniversary.

Jon responded to me right away. This is amazing, considering I was a complete stranger, and he simply wrote "I'm interested."

That started a dialogue about how this could logistically work, and resulted in the following important advice from Jon:

"Your Big Challenge is going to be scheduling everyone. As we are all working cast and crew we can not often guarantee that we will be available on any given day."

Often, your Big Idea begins with a Big Challenge.

Best thing that he could've told me, as I realized I needed to shelve the idea at the time, but not toss it out completely. I thanked Jon for his input and I put it on the shelf.

For 8 years.

The lesson? Timing is Everything.

"Everybody I know has a Big But."

P. W. Herman

"Don't let your Big But get in the way of your Big Idea."

R. T. Richardson

Want to hear another one of my Big Ideas? (Like you have a choice.)

Nostalgia is the future.

Look around you. Vinyl records have returned and are selling more than other formats. Half the shows and movies being released are either reboots or sequels.

Newsflash: *we like to remember things*.

Fans of a band will go to the end of the earth for that band. Fans of a genre will wait until they can get it for free.

When you have a Big Idea, you need to **Find your Fans**.

One of my proudest moments as a manager was when I attended the Cornerstone Festival with my band **Leaderdogs For The Blind**. They had recorded their stellar debut, **Lemonade**, at a Detroit studio frequented by artists including Stevie Wonder and Filter. They then delivered an amazing live set in 100°, July, Illinois heat.

Appropriately, the band's proud parents delivered ice cold lemonade to everybody in the audience and made it a real party. The festival was buzzing about the show for days. As I walked around the grounds that week, many of my jaded music executive friends stopped me and said, "I usually tell all my friends that I like their bands, but I **honestly** am a fan of yours!"

People talked about that show for days, and others stopped by to say they wish they had caught it. I was both the proud papa and the proud soccer mom. We had found our fans.

When my kids were young, I was a freelance writer for several music magazines. This gave me great opportunities to talk to artists as diverse as the legendary Fishbone, The Afters, Pat Boone, Switchfoot,

<u>Bif Naked</u>, TobyMac and more. My kids basically grew up backstage and became such music fans that my daughter used her Christmas money to buy the Beatles' White Album. The salesperson said to her, *"you've given me hope for the next generation"*.

Years later, the kids and I got to see Bif on her acoustic "Stories & Songs tour, and they sang every word, having grown up around her music.

Those backstage experiences helped to instill in them that they could do whatever they wanted to do.

That they could follow their own Big Idea.

Find your fans. They are out there.

Social media makes it much easier to find them. Having said that, it also makes finding them more difficult, as you need to be able to cut through a lot of noise to get their attention.

How can you do that? Be both **Memorable and Easy-To-Find** as you share your Big Idea.

You can do it.

"With Paranormal Activity, Oren Peli showed that you could do this in your house, you could do it with your phone, and it led to so many other great projects from unknown voices."

Sprague Grayden
(24, Paranormal Activity 2)

"Every business and every organization has to have a place online. A central hub for people to find you."

Geoff Laforet
(Laforet Film & Creative)

So, back to "24".

Eight years have passed and I revisit my original idea. What if I could bring together some of the cast and crew of this ground-breaking TV show to celebrate the 20th anniversary of the pilot? Surely, the Fox network would be doing something to commemorate this, right? *Not so much.*

Again, why don't I just do it?

The first step was to come up with a name. Something catchy, something easy to remember, something short and to the point.

Why are each of these things important?

This is the rule I call "Be Easy To Find". It is adapted from one of my favorite books in the world entitled **"Don't Make Me Think."** It is a book about web design and general marketing, and I have found it to be true over and over again. If people have to think too much, once they get to your site, they will move on. Identify what people are looking for and give it to them as quickly as possible.

Case in point. Let me name a few recent movies that you may or may not remember.

Jupiter Ascending

The Changeling

Edge Of Tomorrow

No?

Maybe you will recognize the people that were in them.

Jupiter Ascending (Channing Tatum, Mila Kunis)

The Changeling (Angelina Jolie)

Edge Of Tomorrow (Emily Blunt, Tom Cruise)

In fact, when Edge Of Tomorrow (not a soap opera) released for home viewing, they changed the name to **Live. Die. Repeat.** Very rarely does a film change its name between the theatre and your couch.

The problem was that all three had titles that did absolutely nothing to describe the movie they wanted you to pay to see.

In contrast, I attended a marketing presentation that claimed that the host would reveal the best movie title in all of history. Can you guess what that title was?

The
Texas
Chainsaw
Massacre

Why do you think they chose that title?

OK, I will tell you.

It is simple and to the point, plus it leaves no ambiguity about what you are about to witness. If you take your toddlers' birthday party group to see The Texas Chainsaw Massacre expecting the latest Pixar film, it's kind of on you. The title itself warns you what you are getting into.

Be the Texas Chainsaw Massacre.

Not literally, of course, but take some time to consider your audience and whether they will get what you are doing. Understand that not everybody will. And that is OK.

Also, keep it brief. In the words of the great philosopher Rusty Ryan,

"Never use 7 words when 4 will do."

"You don't need $6 Million to make these movies anymore… everything starts with the story."

Katee Sackhoff
(The Mandalorian, Longmire)

"You felt like you were going to the movie theatre every week!"

Elisha Cuthbert
(24, Happy Endings)

Why do you need a **Big Idea**?

You don't, actually. In fact, many other people around you may never have a Big Idea. That may be OK for them, but remember that they may also be people who remind you of your **Big But**.

The fact that you're reading this at all implies that you do.

Here's another Big Idea: Your Big Idea does not have to be mammoth and/or massively expensive.

So often, the anticipated price tag derails our Big Idea. It becomes our Big But, when it really should not be allowed to.

Need proof?

Every time I start a new class, I like to show the Will Ferrell film **Third Date**. If you haven't watched Third Date, click here and then come back. Please.

For those of you that may have never heard of Will Ferrell, he is kind of a big deal. Not because of his massive ego, a big deal because he has been in major TV shows and films that are known for being funny. You'd be hard pressed to find someone who hasn't watched Elf, Austin Powers or Anchorman. What this means is that Will Ferrell has access to large film budgets, because he has earned that. This short film is the opposite of that. In fact, any one of us could have made Third Date. But we didn't.

As you now know, all he needed was an actress, a PortaJohn, some sound effects and an iPhone. And a genuinely funny idea, of course.

How many of those things do you have access to **right now**?

So although Will Ferrell has the clout to command large budgets, he made Third Date for almost nothing, and it has been viewed millions of times around the world. And it hurts not just a little bit to know that I could have done it first.

But it wasn't my Big Idea.

The NSFW It's Always Sunny In Philadelphia started out with a Big Idea. The show just celebrated its 15th season and became America's longest running live action comedy series. "Sunny" is not the creation of Hollywood insiders or established movie stars, it started with a bunch of friends filming their crazy ideas and putting them on YouTube. There was little to no money at the start. Rob

McElhenny and his team are record-breaking Big Idea people, whether you like the show or not.

Is money your Big But? Is it causing you to stop before you even start? How can you get around that?

I have one option to offer you. **Surround yourself with other Big Idea people**.

"It was a powerful experience at a young age to have some adults in my life who didn't think it was crazy to want to be a writer."

Anna Clark
(The Poisoned City)

We are not meant to live small!"

Kari Pennise-Hummer
(The FeminineXperience)

Why is it important to surround yourself with Big Ideas and Big Idea people?

Take a minute and look around you. There is evidence of Big Ideas everywhere you turn:

- **The iPhone**
- **Your Keurig**
- **It's Always Sunny In Philadelphia**
- **Netflix**

When we were kids, it was the *Rubik's Cube, Cabbage Patch dolls, Fidget Spinners, Gameboys and Blackberrys*.

Since 1996, my personal mission has been to surround myself with creative people.

Growing up in a border city, I got the best of both worlds. There is a quote that states "the average Canadian entrepreneur tries something, and if it doesn't work and they often give up on being an entrepreneur. In contrast, the average American entrepreneur tries something, it doesn't work, and they say 'what's next?'"

This is a massive generalization, but there is some truth to it. I am so grateful that I have both influences, because I favour the American entrepreneurship approach. But, in order to maintain that thought process, I find it important to surround myself with not only Big Idea people, but also highly creative people.

I am not there yet, but my ultimate goal is to **Create more than I Consume**.

Why you may need to ignore the opinions of non-Big Idea people:

- **They are afraid**
- **They are negative**
- **They may not see things the way you do**
- **They are risk-averse**

However, here's why you may need to listen to the opinions of non-Big Idea people:

- They can help you assess the pros and cons
- They may be more pragmatic and realistic
- You have a thick skin, and you won't take it personally

We are at a time when "Zoom" is a universally understood concept. In the world of marketing, a business is successful when they become "Top-of-mind". Good examples are **Google, Kleenex, Band-Aid**. Each one is a brand name accepted as the product name and is often used as a verb.

A great way for your Big Idea to become Top-of-mind is to do things that challenge you, maybe even some that scare you.

When I started my business, I went to the faculty of my college and let them know that I would have more free time available to teach. I agreed to take on more classes as long as the subjects were not outside my areas of expertise, like engineering or medicine. (I do have some limits.) I felt confident about teaching a wide variety of subjects.

Within a week, I received a call that an instructor had bailed at the last minute, and the college needed someone to teach **"Effective Communication"** to a room full of corporate executives for 8 hours.

The following day.

I immediately said "Yes." Then I hung up the phone.

And I freaked out.

But by 8:00 the next morning, I was standing in front of a class full of strangers with an 8-hour lesson plan worked out. I guarantee it wasn't very smooth, but it was interactive and it seemed like the execs had a good time and walked away with the information they came for.

The long-term effect? Bailing out the department that day has led to over **50** additional contracts as a Corporate Trainer.

All because I said "Yes" without over-thinking it.

I needed the challenge. Did I want to call them back immediately and cancel? Of course. But If I had said "No" out of fear, I would've missed both a major opportunity and an ongoing relationship.

That same fear came back on November 5, 2021, but I had already said "Yes".

There was no backing down.

"In life, it is important to take time for strategic planning breaks."

Irene Moore Davis
(Essex County Black Historical Research Society)

"After Buffy wrapped, I got hooked on 24. I remember calling my manager and said, 'I don't care what I have to do, I want to be on this show, it's so good."

D.B. Woodside
(Lucifer, 24)

So… back to "24".

When you have your Big Idea and you have given it a name, I recommend that you first check to see if the domain is available. For me, when I have a Big Idea, I want to own the **dot-com**, also known as the **domain**. I have been using domain.com for years and that is a great place to start.

20yearsof24.com was available

I bought it.

One of the show's catchphrases, EventsOccurInRealTime.com was available.

I bought that too.

With those firmly in hand, I started to put together a plan. I needed to map out how I was going to attain the Big Idea.

For me, that involves **writing it down**. Sometimes, having a plan in front of me makes it seem more real. It also makes me accountable for getting it done.

Why?

I need it to help me focus on my Big Idea. It is important to **Focus on your Big Idea**.

Years before my filmmaker friends Gavin and Sarah moved to Los Angeles, Gavin had made this poster to function as a daily reminder:

This helped him to focus on his Big Idea.

So, this was all happening in the fall of 2019.

In a nutshell, the plan was to confirm 4 to 6 guests from the TV show "24", find a public venue that could accommodate a few hundred people, and reach out to the cast and crew. I had done large events before, mainly music festivals, and I knew it was going to take at least two years to do it well. I also know that I would rather start out with smaller events and build them up, than launch a big event and watch it fail. I learned this from having some huge events fail. Fortunately, I had only been in charge of a few of those. The "field of dreams" approach of 'if you build it, they will come' is not really working in the 21st Century.

Need proof? **Fyre Fest**.

At this point, I had not contacted "24" Director Jon Cassar again, as I needed to get some things in place before I re-started that conversation.

I began some of the groundwork, but not a ton, when March 2020 arrived.

You remember March 2020, when rational people began hoarding toilet paper?

Not our proudest moment.

This is where I learned another valuable lesson.

When you make a plan - make it flexible.

The Great Pause that began in March 2020 threaten to derail my Big Idea. No, it wanted to kill it. Granted, at that point I'd only spent $20 to buy the domains, but I was committed to the plan to build this convention.

Wise words from one of my favorite collaborators and best friends saved my Big Idea...

We got merch!

Reunited and it felt so good…

National coverage from Deadline.com

NEWS TV NEWS

Kiefer Sutherland headlines '24' virtual anniversary event

"I can't wait to talk to you all"

By Seth Webb | 28th October 2021

SECTIONS HOME VIDEO PHOTOS
Kanye West 'Wicked' 'All Too Well' Silk Sonic Mariah Carey Jennifer

Kiefer Sutherland To Headline 20th Anniversary '24' Virtual Reunion

By COREY ATAD 3 Nov 2021 2:52 PM

Kiefer Sutherland in "24" — Photo: Fox-Tv/Kobal/Shutterstock

What Is Your BIG IDEA?

April 2016, The Ark, Ann Arbor, MI

Inside The Bunker Podcast

"The world needs your content."

Remember the <u>Leaderdogs</u> from earlier? After launching their Big Idea in the mid 90s, and recording and playing live, they had put the Big Idea of being a band on the shelf. What I did not realize in March 2020 was that they had taken their Big Idea off of the shelf, and were putting it back in play. In the words of The Blues Brothers, they were *"<u>putting the band back together</u>"*.

The year before, the band had launched a brilliant project called <u>banqupstate</u> and had been very clear that this was not a

Leaderdogs album. I was a fan, and still am, and found out that they had started a podcast called Cheap Flight. They live in three different cities – Milwaukee, Toronto and Dallas and recording a podcast is cheaper than flying. Makes sense, right?

During the initial quarantine, I found myself on my balcony catching up on the Cheap Flight Podcast. I was so engaged that I was actually talking back is if I was in the room with them.

To be clear, that is not how podcasts work, and I got some strange looks from neighbors walking by.

What I found out that day on my balcony, is that the band was taking the Big Idea of **Leaderdogs** back off of the shelf to celebrate their 25th anniversary, and they were drawing straws to figure out who would tell me that I would have to get back to work. I immediately called bandleader Lp and asked if I could join Cheap Flight.

I got bit immediately by the podcast bug.

I had co-hosted The True Groove radio show in Windsor/Detroit for years and had interviewed so many people over the years that podcasting just made sense. All my excuses for not podcasting disappeared when the world cleared my calendar for me. In the course of joining, my good friend Lp said the words that changed the game for me: ***"The World Needs Your Content."***

Within that month, I had joined Cheap Flight as a frequent flyer, and had launched my "People In Your Neighbourhood" Podcast. - conversations with people that I have met over the years that have done and continue to do fascinating things.

Bands, historians, long distance runners, authors - all fascinating people. It's the kind of podcast that my Dad would have done and we have archived some really interesting conversations with so many incredible people. And I continue to do so.

Back to Jack Bauer.

"So they're, like, really interested in you. Will you shave your head?"

Sarah Booth
(Last Call, The Scarehouse)

"Thank God for the commercials. This show is going to give me a heart attack!"

Rodney Charters
(24 Cinematographer)

So what am I now supposed to do with my "24" Convention idea? The world is locked down, and the possibility of doing a physical convention is now out the window, even if we were 18 months in advance.

Those of us that were listening have learned the value of the word *"Pivot"* since the world paused. Things that we wanted to do, we have had to pivot and find new ways to do them.

My Big Idea had to pivot, and again I heard **Lp**'s advice in my ear: *"The World Needs Your Content."*

Podcasting was to be the next natural step for <u>20YearsOf24.com</u>

Why? Everyone at the beginning was at home. Everyone. Remember that place that we used to occasionally stop in to for dinner and sleep? As things changed, we all got to know our homes really well in 2020-21.

Actors and crew that would normally be hard to track down were actually at home waiting for things to open up again.

Aiding in the pivot of my Big Idea was this app called Zoom. Like

Kleenex and Google, Zoom quickly became Top-of-mind.

I have said on many occasions, I wish that in 2019, I had invested in **Zoom and plexiglass**.

In that order.

I have attended many online conferences and meetings in the last 20 years, but honestly, nothing brought the easy-to-use warmth and portability that Zoom did. Remember when I said nostalgia is the future? Agree with me or not, I believe that Zoom took off, partially because it makes us all look like we're in the Brady Bunch end credits.

Why else would people wave every time they leave a Zoom meeting?

Zoom allows guests to participate from the comfort of their own home or office.

So our elevator pitch changed. "Does your client have a phone or a laptop at your home or office? Zoom allows us to have face-to-face conversations with people from the show."

Doors began to open.

Zoom also allows us to pick up on body language cues and our guest engagement levels. All the stuff that I've been teaching about for over 10 years. It was the perfect combination for me.

The next step was to consult **IMDb**, the Internet Movie Database, and find the publicists for some of the actors from the show.

My new pivoted plan was to speak to 8 to 10 cast and crew members from "24" and release them as podcast episodes, maybe once a month, until the anniversary date.

My first two gracious guests were Leslie Hope ("Teri Bauer") and Eric Balfour ("Milo Pressman"). They both made it so easy for me and they were genuinely excited to talk about "24"! I'll always be grateful to them for taking a chance on the "20 Years Of 24" podcast.

I was on the right track, and having Leslie and Eric as guests lent credibility to the other publicists I was talking to.

Then I met Aaron and Justin.

"Don't know anybody in Canada? You do now!"

Lori Baldassi
(Podcaster)

"What is this thing? Can we really do it?"

Howard Gordon
(24 Showrunner)

Next lesson: Your Big Idea benefits from teamwork.

Aaron started the 24 Universe Facebook page, which had about 10,000 followers at the time, and he gave me full authority to promote my Big Idea on his site. Another game changer.

Immediately, Aaron said, "you've got to talk to Justin".

Once I had Aaron's blessing, I posted a casting call of sorts to all the "24" fans in the 24 Universe, that if they could find me a guest from the show, we would co-host that episode together.

Justin responded immediately.

While Aaron is in sunny California, Justin lives just three hours from me in the frozen tundra of Canada. All three of us had an instant rapport, shared fandom and respect for Jack Bauer. Justin's first question was, "would you like to talk to Howard Gordon?" In my film geek head, I thought "Howard Gordon from the X-Files and the guy who launched Homeland? Like that's going to happen."

I fought to suppress that non-Big Idea voice and said "absolutely". Justin then asked for a list of some of the people that I would like to talk to. I remember sending a list of 8 to 10 names, including Jack Bauer himself, Kiefer Sutherland. I had met Kiefer five years before and found him to be easy to talk to, and had hoped that one day, years from now, he might be a guest on our little podcast.

Two days later, Howard Gordon was scheduled to be a guest. Less than 10 days later, Kiefer Sutherland agreed to join us to talk 20 years of "24".

Mind blown.

Needless to say, Justin became my permanent co-host.

The Big Idea that I had over 10 years ago kept getting Bigger and Bigger.

In less than eight months, we talked over 40 cast and crew from the Fox network hit TV show "24", sometimes recording 3 interviews a night. All because of Leslie and Eric's initial interviews and Justin's gentle persistence. If you look at the list of people that we've talked to, you will recognize a team that has collectively gone on to create and lead most of the shows on television and film.

There are far too many insights from our incredible guests to share here (how **Chris Diamantopoulos** got the gig as the voice of Mickey Mouse, **Katie Sackhoff** comparing her roles of Starbuck on Battlestar Galactica and Dana Walsh, how **D.B. Woodside** talked his way onto "24", or how **Carlos Bernard**, who does a spot-on William Devane impression, talked his way out of dying several times), I recommend you dig through our **archives** for lessons that not only apply to acting but to life itself.

Justin and Aaron also helped me build a team as passionate as we were about hosting this crazy thing.

When I was a young concert promoter, I did not understand the term "delegation". I was picking up the band at the airport, feeding them, driving them around, getting them to soundcheck, collecting money at the door. Kids, that is not the way to run a concert. I learned very quickly that I needed to delegate, so that I would keep some level of sanity.

The benefits of having a team, besides camaraderie, are:

- feedback
- support
- constructive criticism, and
- the ability to think outside yourself.

Building this amazing team allowed us to encourage and train the Big Idea people around us. As a result of this push and the increasing availability to stream "24" around the world, the group of 10,000 has grown to 25,000, and we have helped launch great podcasts including Inside The Bunker!

At the end of every interview, we would ask our guest if we could keep them in the loop about our plans for Saturday, November 6, 2021. All but one said yes, even that person turned around and joined us later.

Our plans had to pivot some more.

"I don't want to keep doing this for another 20 years... What if I took that chance?"

Rachel Rose Oginsky
(The Bold & The Beautiful)

"There are possibilities. I did do an Outer Limits & 2 different Twilight Zones."

Xander Berkeley
(T2, The Walking Dead)

Once we realized that we really couldn't hold the physical convention as we had originally planned, we went back to Zoom. In the months leading up, everybody had used Zoom at least once. Right?

Well, almost, but it was clearly Top-of-mind. (There's that word again!)

Our next step was to plan a Zoom Convention. This would allow everyone to appear on screen, from the luxury of their own home, office or film set. Once we decided this would be the venue, I started to look at it from the big picture.

From an event planning stand-point, transportation, hotels and meals are all eliminated.

And, as opposed to a physical convention, any fan in the world could attend. From home. This was truly becoming a **FanDrivenEvent**. Instead of thinking locally, I could think globally.

But for several weeks, nobody was coming.

Except for a small, dedicated group of superfans, Nobody.

How can this be? The 24 Universe group had grown to about 15,000 by that point, and so many claimed that they were interested, but not enough to commit.

The team posted every single day. We tried patreoning, crowdfunding, you name it, we tried it. There had to be a cost to the fans, as we needed both the bandwidth and upgrades to host this event with minimal glitches, but we kept the fee low.

Still.

Nothing.

The event had willing guests (a good problem to have) but Zero traction.

Frustrated, I went back to my team and said "I don't want to host an event that has more guests than fans". Like **Robert DeNiro in Heat**, I was willing to walk away from this Big Idea if we didn't have fan support.

My team was equally shocked by the lack of support. I was done, and I did not want to embarrass us to the guests that believed in us. We had spent months telling them how passionate the "24" Fans were, yet we were seeing little evidence of that passion.

I felt I needed to spend my time more productively.

But… my 24 Convention team listened and talked me through that. They let me vent and then gave their input.

That's one of the many benefits of surrounding yourself with your team of Big Idea people.

I am so grateful they changed my mind and tackled my temporary frustrations… especially after what happened just three days later.

I got **The Call**.

"If the person who could change your dreams is on the other side of that door, what do you have to lose?"

Gavin Michael Booth
(The Scarehouse, Just 20)

"We pushed the limits of what you could show on TV."

Jon Cassar
(Forsaken, The Orville)

Jon Cassar wanted to talk to me.

If Joel and Bob are the fathers of "24", Jon is the cool uncle that keeps track of the family tree and hosts all the barbecues. Now, besides being the first "24" person I'd contacted all those years before, Jon had been a guest on the podcast a few months before.

One of the great thrills of that conversation was that Jon had asked to keep it going. I always keep to the time limits requested by the guest or their publicist, and my standard line is "we want to be mindful of your schedule", to which Jon responded "I'm having fun with you guys!"

The last thing I ever want to do is overstay my welcome.

Since Jon had been so easy to talk to, I was happy to respond.

This time, his first question was "what's the plan for this convention? Everyone is asking me, and I told them I'd find out." When I explained that we wanted people to connect with worldwide fans and their colleagues from the comfort of home, in the form of a few panel discussions, he was again interested.

Jon gave me the next great piece of advice: "partner with a charity we are passionate about, and I'll get more people on board."

We did, and he kept his word.

With this advice, Justin had recommended that we reach out to Operation Smile Canada. With three short weeks left to go, Operation Smile agreed to partner with us and put their full support behind this wild event. An event that had never been done.

Once that partnership was in place, Jon began to contact everybody he knew in the "24" world, and all of a sudden, we had people contacting us, asking us if they could get involved on November 6. I won't name names, but a few actually came out of retirement/sabbatical to spend the day with us.

Unbelievable.

The "24" cast and crew are Big Idea people.

And once again, Kiefer Sutherland, Jack Bauer himself, agreed to join us on the day. Once that was confirmed, Justin went about looking for a media partner to announce Kiefer's involvement. After being passed on by several,

Justin secured Deadline.com to help us get the word out. I have been reading **Deadline** for years and even my Big Idea mind couldn't believe it. Nellie Andreeva took our media release and put it on the front page for the world to see.

This taught me that I could **Look Global, Then Think Local**.

As a result of all of these efforts, we went from 20 hardcore "24" fans to 240 fans registered in less than 2 weeks, with over 40 cast and crew on 8 panels. This group collectively represented 22 countries.

Actually, it quickly turned into 9 panels. So many of the "24" cast and crew had previously worked together on the Canadian show *La Femme Nikita*, that I got another Call. "24" creator Joel Surnow asked if we could add a "Nikita" panel at the beginning.

To paraphrase Ivan Reitman's Ghostbusters, when a guy as nice as Joel asks you if you would add a panel, "you say Yes!"

I wrote down this lesson as soon as it came to me. "**To successfully take your Big Idea to the next level, you need a Lightning Rod**."

Jon Cassar was our lightning rod. And our patient guide for the last few weeks.

Just be careful what you wish for.

"I got a call from my agent and she said 'hey, can you get to a fax?"

Sarah Clarke
(Twilight, Bosch)

"We've been embedded at Marvel Studios for 4 years. We were on the set of Endgame and Infinity War. We just had a crazy, crazy experience doing that."

Tara Bennett
(Lost Encyclopedia)

When you experience a 1200% increase in registration, the stakes escalate as well. I had done Zoom conferences for up to 100 people, but never the size that the "24" Convention had grown to. With each registration, I wondered, "have I gotten in over my head?"

The answer I heard in my head was "Absolutely."

Which brings me back to "Effective Communication". If I had not said "Yes", I would have lost out on years of amazing and unique teaching opportunities (and also income). Because I said yes to a class I had never taught, I taught a group of 50 students from Panama for a full year. I would've never gotten that experience or learned so much about the beautifully diverse people of Panama.

So as I inwardly panicked how about balancing a myriad of time zones and personalities, I remembered another Big Ideal lesson:

Embrace The Free.

I once wrote an article for musicians entitled "PLFS - People Love Free Stuff". That statement is even more true today.

If you don't know how to do something, look for it on YouTube. It's there.

Or try LearnStuffOnZoom.com

If you want to find more Big Idea people to encourage you, watch a Ted Talk. Watch 5 - they're free! If you need help finding the right one, join us for Third Thursday Ted Talk each month.

So, after I upgraded my software and hardware for the Big Day, I went to YouTube University. My team and I devoured many tutorials on how to make this event the best it could possibly be.

Having said that...

Perfection was not the goal of the event. We promised our guests and fans that it would not be flawless or perfect, but that it would be fun and entertaining.

And most importantly, on schedule. I Hate Late.

There were several nights in late October and November, on the few times I did sleep, that I dreamt of power outages and myself curled up in a corner, overwhelmed by the scope of this event. But there was also adrenaline in those moments.

The feeling that I was doing the craziest thing I had ever done in my life.

That it would be either a rousing success or a colossal failure. Both excited me equally in those moments.

It was my Big Idea and it was about to launch live.

Not even SNL runs for 9 hours.

What was I thinking?

"The first thing Joey The Jerk says to me is, 'man, you need to write a book.'"

Christopher Cooper
(Soup The Chemist)

"Mike Judge just looked at me and went, 'keep doing exactly what you're doing.'"

Chris Diamantopoulos
(Red Notice, True Story)

I needed to listen to the <u>People In My Neighbourhood</u>.

So, I reached out.

In the last few weeks before the convention, as I was losing my mind, my friend Gavin put me in touch with his friend <u>**Rob**</u>. Rob gave me the greatest piece of advice. He said "some people will be nervous using Zoom, why don't you make yourself available the night before, in case anybody wants to log in and make sure they could connect?". I hadn't thought about that. I figured everybody in the world was comfortable with Zoom at this point. I was dead wrong.

On the night before, I created a two-hour window where I would sit and wait for anybody who wanted to test the Zoom link first. In those two hours, we had a mini-Convention. Over a dozen guests showed up and started talking to each other, reconnecting and exchanging contact information.

What I didn't anticipate is that this "test run" also put my mind at ease. Even though I was functioning on little to no sleep, I had a feeling that the next day was going to work. Not smoothly, not perfectly, but I saw that people were happy to be in the same virtual room together for the first time in years. If I had slept at all that night, it would have been a restful sleep.

"For you to allow us into your living room? That's a big deal. That you're able to share this moment with them, if you tell the story right, you can move mountains."

Tzi Ma
(Rush Hour, Kung Fu)

"The following takes place between 5 pm and 6 pm."

Kiefer Sutherland
(24, The Lost Boys, Stand By Me, Forsaken, Flatliners, A Few Good Men….)

So… how did Saturday, November 6, 2021 go?

The easiest answer? A Big Love Fest. But do not just take my word.

Allow me to share some of the comments from our esteemed guests:

"Thank you both for bringing this wonderful event to life. You guys did a brilliant job. It meant so much to all of us to get all the love we received today. A great reunion and hopefully a fun time for the fans. Be well, gents..."

Joel Surnow, "24" Co-Creator

"You pulled off a logistical masterpiece. Bravo. I could not have imagined a better way to reconnect with my fellow show-mates and the fans."

Michael Loceff, "24" Writer

"Thank you, Ryan - it really was great. 24 was a meaningful experience for everyone involved; and it was evident in the fact that we all still have such fondness and appreciation for each other. So grateful you put it together to mark the anniversary!"

Howard Gordon, "24" Showrunner

"Well done today! Thank you for having me and thank you for

organizing it! I hope the fans enjoyed it as much as I did."

Elisha Cuthbert ("Kim Bauer")

"You guys rock! You did a beautiful thing by bringing us all together where we could enjoy each other's company and catch up, and giving fans a long overdue chance to get inside the world of 24."

Nick Jameson, ("President Yuri Suvarov")

"It was great connecting with you and being a part of the 24 anniversary convention".

Adoni Maropis ("Abu Fayed")

"What a fun day! Thank you for everything."

Joseph Hodges, "24" Production Designer

"Thanks so much for pulling this all together!"

Leslie Hope ("Teri Bauer")

"Classy walk down a lane of great memories. Thanks so much Justin and Ryan and all who helped you turn this into a beautiful day. I'm in NOLA missing my family, but so nice to connect with the extended Nikita/24 family. This convention could have been hours longer...."

Carlo Rota ("Morris O'Brian")

"Too short. We need to do it in person!!!"

Carlos Bernard ("Tony Almeida")

"It was a wonderful day!"

Jim Lapidus. "24" Costume Designer

"Congratulations on pulling off such a giant event."

Stephen Hopkins, "24" Pilot Director

Thank you – really enjoyed myself. Take care."

Kiefer Sutherland ("Jack Bauer")

Wow.

The genuine excitement of our guests to reconnect that I caught a glimpse of the night before was magnified at least 24x at the event. People who had not seen each other for almost 20 years were thrilled to be together again. People who had never met told each other how much they respected their work. People fondly remembered the team members that had passed on with great respect.

And the Family atmosphere that we had been hearing about, from so many angles on our podcast, was on full display that day.

That's what happened.

We started on time, we ended on time.

No panels ran overtime.

Our moderators, who were also Superfans, were exceptional.

Our gracious guests helped us to raise funds that paid for **28** cleft lip and palate surgeries for children around the world.

I won't say too much more about the day,

a) because it was a blur for me,

and

b) it is available for you to watch at

EventsOccurInRealTime.com

See the day in all its glory, for yourself.

And there was **No Ego** in the room all day.

Zero.

And I **Lived Another Day**, even though I barely remember the afterparty.

Also, I forgot how to use a tablet and phone for 2 days after.

Literally. My brain enjoyed a badly needed vacation.

We reunited Jack Bauer and his Family.

This is the story of one of my **Big Ideas** that turned out far better than I could have dreamed.

The world needs your Big Idea.

PREVIOUSLY ON 24..

- ✓ Ask. Ask. Ask.

- ✓ Get Past Your Big But

- ✓ Find Your Fans

- ✓ Be Memorable And Easy-To-Find

- ✓ Write Out Your Big Idea

- ✓ Make Your Plan Flexible

- ✓ Surround Yourself With Other Big Idea People

- ✓ Build Your Team

- ✓ Consider A Charitable Partner
- ✓ Your Big Idea May Require A Big Challenge
- ✓ Find Your Lightning Rod
- ✓ Look Global Then Think Local
- ✓ Embrace The Free
- ✓ The World Needs Your Big Idea

...A FEW FINAL LESSONS...

Make and sell the T-shirt

Don't be afraid to ask for help

Record everything

Follow up

Enjoy the moment

Be grateful.

Aim your camera if you choose to
"pay-what-it's-worth-to-you".

*Thank you again for taking
the time to think about your
Big Idea!*

www.ingramcontent.com/pod-product-compliance
Lightning Source LLC
Chambersburg PA
CBHW020318290526
45785CB00007B/2830